LEGENDARY LIVES

I0896432

Bessie Coleman

by Betsy Rathburn
Illustrated by Claudia Marianno

BLASTOFF! MISSIONS

BLASTOFF! MISSIONS, AN IMPRINT OF BELLWETHER MEDIA BY FLUTTERBEE

Blastoff! Missions takes you on a learning adventure! Colorful illustrations and exciting narratives highlight cool facts about our world and beyond. Read the mission goals and follow the narrative to gain knowledge, build reading skills, and have fun!

Traditional Nonfiction

Narrative Nonfiction

Blastoff! Universe

MISSION GOALS

> FIND YOUR SIGHT WORDS IN THE BOOK.

> LEARN ABOUT BESSIE COLEMAN'S LIFE.

> LEARN HOW BESSIE COLEMAN FOUGHT AGAINST SEGREGATION.

This edition first published in 2026 by Bellwether Media, Inc.

Text copyright © 2026 by Bellwether Media, Inc. All rights reserved. No part of this publication may be reproduced, stored in any retrieval system, or transmitted in any form or by any means, electronic, mechanical, photocopying, recording, or otherwise, without written permission of the publisher.

BLASTOFF! MISSIONS and associated logos are trademarks and/or registered trademarks of Bellwether Media, Inc. Bellwether Media is a division of FlutterBee Education Group.

For information regarding permission, write to Bellwether Media, Inc., Attention: Permissions Department, 3500 American Blvd W, Suite 150, Bloomington, MN 55431.

Library of Congress Cataloging-in-Publication Data is available at www.loc.gov or upon request from the publisher.

ISBN: 9798893048421 (hardcover)
ISBN: 9798898800161 (paperback)
ISBN: 9798893049428 (ebook)

Editor: Rebecca Sabelko Designer: Andrea Schneider

Printed in the United States of America, North Mankato, MN.

This is **Blastoff Jimmy**! He is here to help you on your mission and share fun facts along the way!

Table of Contents

Flying High

Bessie Coleman flies high! She is in an **air show**.

Below, the crowd cheers and claps as she flies in a big loop. People are amazed by Bessie's **stunts**!

doing a stunt

Taking Off

It is the late 1800s. Bessie lives with her family in Texas.

She likes to play outside with her 12 brothers and sisters.

It is 1898. Bessie goes to a **segregated** school. There is little money for books or paper.

Bessie likes to learn. She is good at math!

Ready to Soar

Bessie lives in Chicago. She works as a **manicurist**.

Bessie dreams of flying an airplane. But there are no places for Black women to learn in the United States.

It is 1921. Bessie trains at a flight school in France. It is **dangerous**. But she loves to fly.

She learns many tricks. She earns a flying **license**.

JIMMY SAYS

Bessie was the first American to earn a license to fly anywhere in the world.

Lifting Others

Bessie is back in the U.S. No businesses will hire a Black woman **pilot**.

Instead, Bessie travels to air shows. She wows crowds with **figure eights** and **barrel rolls**.

doing a barrel roll
Look!

It is 1925. Bessie does air shows and **lectures** in Texas. She speaks out against segregation.

JIMMY SAYS

Bessie dreamt of opening her own flying school. She wanted to make it easier for Black people to learn to fly.

Today, she jumps from a plane. She lands in the middle of the crowd!

Bessie plans to fly in a show in her hometown. But the entrance gate is segregated.

She does not fly until Black and white guests can use the same gate.

WHITES

It is 1936. Today is the **anniversary** of Bessie's death. Black pilots drop flowers on her grave.

Bessie is remembered for her support of the Black community. She is an aviation **pioneer**!

Bessie Coleman Profile

Born

January 26, 1892,
in Atlanta, Texas

Died

April 30, 1926

Accomplishments

First Black American woman pilot and first American to earn a license to fly anywhere in the world

Timeline

1898: begins attending school

1915: moves to Chicago and begins working as a manicurist

1920: moves to France to attend a flying school

1921: earns her license to fly and moves back to the U.S.

1922: gives her first lecture on flying

Glossary

air show–an event where pilots do tricks in airplanes

anniversary–the date that something took place in a year before it

barrel rolls–tricks where an airplane makes one complete roll by circling around its flight path

dangerous–able to cause injury or harm

figure eights–tricks where an airplane flies in a pattern shaped like the number eight

lectures–talks to teach people about something

license–a document that gives permission to do something

manicurist–a person who cares for hands and fingernails

pilot–a person who flies a plane

pioneer–a person who is the first to do something

segregated–set apart based on race

stunts–tricks

To Learn More

AT THE LIBRARY

Beevor, Lucy. *The Invention of the Airplane.* North Mankato, Minn.: Capstone Press, 2018.

London, Martha. *Bessie Coleman: Bold Pilot Who Gave Women Wings.* North Mankato, Minn.: Capstone Press, 2021.

Spiller, Sara. *Bessie Coleman.* Ann Arbor, Mich.: Cherry Lake Publishing, 2019.

ON THE WEB

FACTSURFER

Factsurfer.com gives you a safe, fun way to find more information.

1. Go to www.factsurfer.com.
2. Enter "Bessie Coleman" into the search box and click 🔍.
3. Select your book cover to see a list of related content.

BEYOND THE MISSION

> WHAT FACT FROM THE BOOK DID YOU THINK WAS THE MOST INTERESTING?

> WHAT QUESTIONS WOULD YOU HAVE ASKED BESSIE ABOUT HER LIFE?

> WHY DO YOU THINK BESSIE IS AN IMPORTANT PERSON TO LEARN ABOUT?

Index

45th Parallel Press

Ann Arbor, Michigan

www.cherrylakepublishing.com

Content Adviser: Liv Williams, Editor, iLivExtreme

Reading Adviser: Beth Walker Gambro, MS, Ed., Reading Consultant, Yorkville, IL

Photo Credits: © Sinesp/Shutterstock, cover, title page; © Wisarut pumipak/Shutterstock, 5; © Tatiana Kovaleva/Shutterstock, 6; © Evan Linnell/iStock.com, 7; © Pictorial Press Ltd/Alamy, 8; © Flavio Almeida/Shutterstock, 9; © Muslianshah Masrie/Shutterstock, 11; © Darminladiro/Shutterstock, 13; © Doug Blane/BASE Jumping/Alamy, 15; © frantic00/Shutterstock, 16–17; © Huntstyle/ Shutterstock, 18; © Abbie Warnock-Matthews/Shutterstock, 21; © Kelly vanDellen/Shutterstock, 22; © givaga/Shutterstock, 25; © cwhy25/Shutterstock, 26; © Anze Furlan/Shutterstock, 28; © Giovanni Seabra/Dreamstime.com, 29

Copyright © 2026 by Cherry Lake Publishing
All rights reserved. No part of this book may be reproduced or utilized in any form or by any means without written permission from the publisher.

Library of Congress Cataloging-in-Publication Data has been filed and is available at catalog.loc.gov

Cherry Lake Press would like to acknowledge the work of the Partnership for 21st Century Learning, a Network of Battelle for Kids. Please visit Battelle for Kids online for more information.

Printed in the United States of America

Note from publisher: Websites change regularly, and their future contents are outside of our control. Supervise children when conducting any recommended online searches for extended learning opportunities.

ABOUT THE AUTHOR

Virginia Loh-Hagan is an author, university professor, former classroom teacher, and curriculum designer. In college, she jumped off a bunk bed and broke her toe. No more jumping for her. She lives in San Diego with her very tall husband and very naughty dogs.

SHRED IT!

LIFE ON THE EDGE

EXTREME BASE JUMPING

Virginia Loh-Hagan